PRAYER
STUDY GUIDE

The Power of a
PRAYING®
PARENT

STORMIE
OMARTIAN

HARVEST HOUSE PUBLISHERS
EUGENE, OREGON

Cover by Koechel Peterson & Associates, Minneapolis, Minnesota

THE POWER OF A PRAYING® PARENT PRAYER AND STUDY GUIDE

Copyright © 2000 by Stormie Omartian
Published by Harvest House Publishers
Eugene, Oregon 97402
www.harvesthousepublishers.com

ISBN-13: 978-0-7369-1981-4
ISBN-10: 0-7369-1981-3

Printed in the United States of America

08 09 10 11 12   / BP / 10 9 8 7 6 5 4 3

A supplemental workbook to
The Power of a Praying Parent
by Stormie Omartian,
for those interested in practical
group or individual study.

Contents

How Do I Begin? ⌒ 7

WEEK 1: Becoming a Praying Parent ⌒ 11

WEEK 2: Releasing My Child into God's Hands ⌒ 21

WEEK 3: Securing Protection from Harm ⌒ 25

WEEK 4: Feeling Loved and Accepted ⌒ 31

WEEK 5: Establishing an Eternal Future ⌒ 37

WEEK 6: Honoring Parents and Resisting Rebellion ⌒ 41

WEEK 7: Maintaining Good Family Relationships ⌒ 47

WEEK 8: Attracting Godly Friends and Role Models ⌒ 53

WEEK 9: Developing a Hunger for the Things of God ⌒ 59

WEEK 10: Being the Person God Created ⌒ 65

WEEK 11: Following Truth, Rejecting Lies ⌒ 71

WEEK 12: Enjoying a Life of Health and Healing ⌒ 77

WEEK 13: Having the Motivation for Proper Body Care ⌒ 81

WEEK 14: Instilling the Desire to Learn ⌒ 87

WEEK 15: Identifying God-Given Gifts and Talents ⌒ 91

WEEK 16: Learning to Speak Life ⌒ 97

WEEK 17: Staying Attracted to Holiness and Purity ⌒ 101

WEEK 18: Praying Through a Child's Room ⌒ 107

WEEK 19: Enjoying Freedom from Fear ⌒ 113

WEEK 20: Receiving a Sound Mind ⌒ 119

WEEK 21: Inviting the Joy of the Lord ⌒ 125

WEEK 22: Destroying an Inheritance of Family Bondage ⁓ 131

WEEK 23: Avoiding Alcohol, Drugs, and Other Addictions ⁓ 137

WEEK 24: Rejecting Sexual Immorality ⁓ 143

WEEK 25: Finding the Perfect Mate ⁓ 149

WEEK 26: Living Free of Unforgiveness ⁓ 155

WEEK 27: Walking in Repentance ⁓ 161

WEEK 28: Breaking Down Ungodly Strongholds ⁓ 167

WEEK 29: Seeking Wisdom and Discernment ⁓ 173

WEEK 30: Growing in Faith ⁓ 179

Answers to Prayer ⁓ 183

How Do I Begin?

*W*elcome to the wonderful and fulfilling task of be-coming an effective praying parent. While it is easy for every mom and dad to have the desire to pray for their child, knowing *how* to pray specifically can often be a challenge. That's because each child is unique. What works for one may not work for another. And with each age, there are new challenges and concerns. At one point they are too young to tell you what is going on in their lives, at another they don't *want* to tell you what is going on in their lives. And once they reach adulthood, you never really know what is going on in their lives. Prayer is the only solution. The good news is that God has given you the authority to intercede powerfully for your child no matter what age he (she) is or whether he (she) lives with you or not. And He will give you the revelation you need to pray on target. This workbook is intended to as-sist you in that.

What You'll Need

This PRAYER AND STUDY GUIDE is divided into a 30-week plan for use in personal or group study. You will need to have my book THE POWER OF A PRAYING PARENT to read along with this. The answers to many of the questions will be found in it. You will also need a Bible. I have quoted the New King James Version here, but you can use whatever translation you want. Just make sure the Bible you have is easy for you to understand, and one you feel free to write in.

About Your Answers

Many of the questions in this PRAYER AND STUDY GUIDE will have to be answered separately for each individual child. If you are praying for more than one child, you will not have room in this book for all of your answers. In that case, it would be beneficial to keep your responses in a notebook or journal. The answers are not for anyone else to read, and you will not be tested on them. They are to help you determine how to pray specifically for each child. This kind of prayer notebook for your children is wonderful to keep and look back on years later. You will be amazed at how strategically the Lord directed you to pray and how He answered those prayers.

Try to answer all the questions and follow the directions to the best of your ability. Even if your child is an infant, or he (she) is grown and has been gone from your home for some time, God will reveal things to you about him (her) with regard to the questions. Try to write something for each entry. If nothing else, write what is in your heart regarding that question. When instructed to write out a prayer, it doesn't have to be a lengthy one. Two or three sentences will cover the subject of focus.

How to Proceed

In group study, it's good to follow the order of this book so that everyone will literally be on the same page when they come together each week. In individual study, you do not have to proceed in the same order if there are more pressing concerns that need to be addressed immediately. In any case, however, Chapter One and Chapter Two of THE POWER OF A PRAYING PARENT should be read before proceeding on to any others.

In a Group

When studying in a group, read the appropriate chapter in THE POWER OF A PRAYING PARENT and answer the questions in the corresponding chapter here in the PRAYER AND STUDY GUIDE on your own. When the group comes together, the leader will go over the questions and discuss what insights God has given each person as he or she feels led to share them. This will be the perfect time to pray as a group for your children. Group intercession for children is very powerful, so take advantage of every opportunity to pray for them in this way.

How to Pray a Scripture

Frequently you will be asked to write out a specific scripture as a prayer over yourself or your child. This is to help you learn to include the Word of God in your prayers. Also, there is power in writing out your prayers. To help you understand how to do that, I have included an example of how I pray Ephesians 6:10-11 over my daughter. Look it up in your Bible and see how I have personalized it:

> "I pray that Mandy will be strong in You, Lord, and move in Your power. I pray that she will be able to put on the whole armor of God. I pray that Mandy will be able to stand strong against the wiles of the devil."

Your Role

Your role is to become an intercessor for your child. *An intercessor is one who prays for someone and makes possible the ability of that person to respond to God.* No one else on earth will ever pray for your child with the fervency and consistency that you will. What an awesome opportunity to powerfully affect your child's life for eternity.

WEEK ONE

Read Chapter 1: "Becoming a Praying Parent"
from THE POWER OF A PRAYING PARENT

1. List three traits you see as your child's best qualities.

   SENSITIVE/KIND-HEARTED
   ORGANIZED
   VERY CAREFUL

2. How could these good qualities become liabilities if
   they are not covered in prayer?

   BECOME A FOLLOWER
   CAN CAUSE FRUSTRATION/ANGER
   SCARED AND RELUCTANT

3. List the three biggest concerns you have for your child.   GETTING SICK - MOSTLY CANCER

    NOT BEING CHALLENGED

    COORDINATION SKILLS

    NOT HAVING A SIBLING

    OUTSIDE INFLUENCES

4. Do you ever feel overwhelmed by any of these concerns? __YES__ . In what way?

    CONSUMING MY LIFE

    BEING A FOLLOWER WITH OTHER CHILDRENS
    ACTIONS

5. Does your child have any negative character traits that need to be covered in prayer? _____ . What are they?

6. How could these negative traits be turned into positive qualities or assets in your child's life? (For example, a child's tendency to dominate other children could be tempered by the love of God, mixed with a heart of compassion, and turned into a great leadership quality.)

BECOME SENSITIVE "MAN"

7. Look up James 4:7 and underline it in your Bible. Who are you supposed to resist? __THE DEVIL__. When you resist, what will happen? __HE WILL FLEE__. Do you believe that you can successfully resist the enemy's plans for your children in prayer? __YES__. Why or why not?

BY CONTINUING TO PRAY FOR HIM REMEBERING WHAT HE HAS DONE IN MY LIFE

8. Read Deuteronomy 32:30 and underline it in your Bible. According to this, how many of the enemy's forces can you cause to flee when you pray? _____ __10,000_____. How many when you pray with one other person? __1,000_____. Do you believe there is power in praying with other believers for your children? __YES____. Why or why not?

> PATTI PRAYS FOR CALEB AND US
> ALL THE TIME - VERY POWERFUL

9. In what ways do you feel you have done a good job as a parent?

> ~~[crossed out]~~
> KEPT HIM SAFE AND COVERED IN LOVE
> BEING CONSISTIENT
> TAUGHT HIM COMPASSION

10. Do you feel you have ever made any mistakes as a parent? __YES__. If so, list what they are and what would you have done differently. Then write out a prayer asking God to redeem those situations.

REACTING WITHOUT THINKING FROM LACK OF PATICENCE

11. Do you ever feel guilt as a parent? __YES__. Why or why not? (All parents at one time or another feel guilt about something regarding their children. The purpose of this question is not to make you feel bad, but rather to identify this area so that the devil can't use it against you.)

NOT BEING ABLE TO GIVE HIM A SIBLING

12. Is there anything you would like to change about yourself or your life that would alleviate the guilt you feel as a parent? _____. Explain your answer. Write a prayer asking God to help you make the changes.

13. Do you feel that you generally expect a lot of yourself? __YES__. Do you expect yourself to be a perfect parent? __SOMETIMES__. Explain your answer.

    WHEN HE ACTS A CERTAIN WAY - I
    FEEL LIKE IT REFLECTS ON MY
    PARENTING

14. Read Romans 8:1 and underline it in your Bible. How are we to walk in order to be free of feeling condemnation? <u>WITH CHRIST - <s>80</s></u> . How are we *not* to walk? <u>WITHOUT CHRIST - IN THE FLESH</u> Write a prayer asking God to help you walk free of condemnation.

15. Read Ephesians 6:12-13 and underline it in your Bible. Whom are we wrestling against when we pray? <u>SPIRTUAL FORCES OF EVIL AND THE DARK WORLD</u> . What are we supposed to do to withstand them? <u>PUT ON OUR ARMOR</u> . Write out a prayer asking God to help you do that, especially with regards to your children.

16. Read 1 Peter 5:8-9 and underline it in your Bible. Who is your enemy and the enemy of your children? __THE DEVIL__. What is he constantly doing? __LOOKING FOR SOMEONE TO DEVOUR__. What are you to do in response?

    BE ALERT AND RESIST HIM

    BE SELF-CONTROLLED

17. Read Luke 10:19 and underline it in your Bible. God has given you authority over all __POWER OF THE ENEMY__. That means for your children as well as yourself. Do you see the enemy trying to threaten your child in any way? _____. If so, in what way?

18. Read John 15:5 and underline it in your Bible. How does this verse apply to you as a parent? ~~He~~ HE IS __THE VINE - I AM BRANCHES__. Are you able to fully depend on God to help you raise your children?

    I AM ABLE - NEED TO RELY ON HIM MORE

19. Read 1 Peter 4:8. What will cover the places where we miss the mark as parents? ___LOVE___ .
Write out a prayer asking God to help you love your child with such unconditional love that it smooths all the rough places, heals all wounds, and covers your weaknesses.

20. Pray out loud the prayer on page 30 in THE POWER OF A PRAYING PARENT. Include any specifics about yourself as a parent.

WEEK TWO

Read Chapter 2: "Releasing My Child into God's Hands"
from THE POWER OF A PRAYING PARENT

1. Are you highly protective of your child to the point
   that you constantly worry over his (her) safety?
   ___*NO*___. Explain why or why not.

   I KNOW THAT I AM NOT IN
   CONTROL.

2. Read 1 Peter 5:6-7 and underline it in your Bible.
   What are you supposed to do with your cares and
   concerns for your child? *GIVE THEM TO*
   *GOD*___. Are you able to easily do that?

   NOT ALL THE TIME

3. Do you believe God is a good Father and that He loves your child even more than you do? __YES__. Explain why you do or do not believe that.

    MY CHILD IS A GIFT GIVEN TO ME

4. Have you asked God to be in control of your life? __YES__. Of your child's life? __NO__. Why or why not?

    ME - I NEEDED HIM

    CHILD - "FORGET" TO PRAY FOR HIM

5. Where does prayer for your child begin?_____
    __GIVING IT TO GOD__.
    Releasing your child into God's hands is a sign of __FAITH AND TRUST__.
    (See page 36 of THE POWER OF A PRAYING PARENT.)

6. Do you believe that when you release your child to God, he (she) will be in good hands? __YES__. Why or why not?

> HE WANTS ALL THE THINGS I WANT
> - FOR CALEB

7. Is there any reason why it would be difficult for you to fully release your child into God's hands? __NO__. Explain your answer.

> ITS A MATTER OF REMINDING
> MYSELF THAT HE IS IN CONTROL

8. Read Isaiah 65:23 and underline it in your Bible. Put a star next to it. Write it out below as a proclamation and claim it as a promise for your child. ("I do not labor in vain. I did not bring forth *name of child* for trouble...")

> I DO NOT LABOR IN VAIN. I DID NOT
> BRING FORTH CALEB IN TROUBLE.
> I AM BLESSED BY THE LORD AND
> CALEB WILL BE BLESSED TOO.

9. Read Psalm 127:3 and underline it in your Bible. Do
    you believe your child is a blessing from God?
    __YES__. Why or why not?

    ~~PRAY~~ HE IS A REWARD FROM GOD.

10. Pray out loud the prayer on pages 36–37 of THE
    POWER OF A PRAYING PARENT. Include specifics God
    has revealed about you or your child.

WEEK THREE

Read Chapter 3: "Securing Protection from Harm"
from THE POWER OF A PRAYING PARENT

1. What are the greatest dangers that most concern you
   for your child?

2. Write out a prayer asking God to protect your child
   specifically from those things which most concern
   you.

3. Do you believe that God can protect your child from those dangers? _____. Why or why not?

4. Read Psalm 112:1-8 and underline it in your Bible. What does God promise to those who reverence and obey Him?

5. According to Psalm 112:1, are you the kind of person who is a candidate for God's blessings? _____. Why or why not?

6. Does your child ever express fear for his (her) own safety? _____. Do you believe this is a valid fear? _____. Why or why not? How could you pray with and for your child concerning this fear?

7. Write out a prayer asking God to reveal to you any hidden dangers that you do not see. When He shows them to you, write them down and add them to your prayer list for your child.

8. Write out a prayer asking God to show you anything you need to do to increase your child's safety. Then ask Him to give you peace about it.

9. Read Psalm 61:1-5 and underline it in your Bible. Put a star next to verses 3 and 4. Write these two verses as a prayer over your child. ("Lord, I pray that You will be a shelter for *name of child* ...")

10. Pray out loud the prayer on pages 43–44 in THE POWER OF A PRAYING PARENT. Include specifics about the protection of your child.

WEEK FOUR

Read Chapter 4: "Feeling Loved and Accepted"
from THE POWER OF A PRAYING PARENT

1. Read Isaiah 41:9-10 and underline it in your Bible.
   Do you believe that you are chosen and accepted by
   God? _____. Do you believe God will
   strengthen, help, and uphold you? _____.
   Why or why not?

2. Do you believe Isaiah 41:9-10 is true for your child?
   _____. Write a prayer asking God to help
   your child believe that he (she) is chosen by God
   and that God will always be with him (her).

3. How much do you love your child? Explain.

4. Have you told your child how much you love him (her)? _____. Are you certain your child perceives and believes that you love him (her) the way you said you do? _____. Explain.

5. Did you feel loved as a child? _____. Do you think your experiences as a child have influenced the way you show love to your child? _____. How so?

6. What can you do for your child today that will make him (her) feel loved? (If you don't know, ask God to show you and ask your child to tell you.)

7. Does your child generally feel accepted or rejected by people outside the family? _____.
   If you don't know, ask God to reveal that to you and ask your child to tell you. How could you pray about that?

8. Are there specific or isolated situations in your child's life when he (she) feels rejection? _____ _____. Do you think this is a real concern, or has your child believed something that has no basis in truth? _____.
   How could you pray specifically about that?

9. Do you believe your child ever fears being rejected in certain social situations? _____. Write out a prayer which you could pray over your child whenever he (she) is about to enter an uncomfortable social situation.

10. Pray out loud the prayer on pages 49–50 of THE POWER OF A PRAYING PARENT. Include specifics related to you and your child.

WEEK FIVE

Read Chapter 5: "Establishing an Eternal Future"
from THE POWER OF A PRAYING PARENT

1. Read John 6:40 and underline it in your Bible. Do
   you believe what Jesus says here is true? _____.
   In light of this verse, what is the most important
   thing you can pray about for your child?

2. Has your child received Jesus as his (her) Savior?
   _____. If not, write a prayer about that. If
   yes, write a prayer asking for his (her) relationship to
   grow deeper.

3. How would you describe your relationship with God?
   _____.
   How do you think that affects your child's relationship with God? _____
   _____. How could
   you pray about that?

4. Are you able to talk freely with your child about your
   relationship with God? _____. What is his
   (her) response?

5. Does your child talk openly and freely with you and others about his (her) relationship with God? _____. How could you pray about that?

6. Read John 14:12-14 and underline it in your Bible. Put a star next to verse 14. What does this verse mean to you?

7. What is the promise in verse 14 for your child if he (she) believes in Jesus? _____

_____.

Does your child believe this?

8. Is there anything you could tell your child about the Lord's goodness to you that would inspire him (her) to draw closer to God or to love God more? Write it here, and then tell him (her) at your first opportunity.

9. According to page 56 in THE POWER OF A PRAYING PARENT, what should be a parent's ongoing prayer? Write that out as a prayer below.

10. Pray out loud the prayer on pages 56–57 in THE POWER OF A PRAYING PARENT. Include specifics that relate to your child.

WEEK SIX

Read Chapter 6:
"Honoring Parents and Resisting Rebellion"
from THE POWER OF A PRAYING PARENT

1. Read Ephesians 6:1-3 and underline it in your Bible. In light of these verses, why is it important for you to teach your child to honor you as the parent? What could happen if you don't?

2. The idols in a child's heart that lead him (her) into rebellion are _____ and _____. (See page 60 of

THE POWER OF A PRAYING PARENT.) Do you ever recognize either of those in your child? If so, write out a prayer that they be broken in your child's personality. If no, write out a prayer that they do not gain a foothold in his (her) life.

3. The opposite of rebellion is _____.
The first step of obedience for children is _____
_____. (See page 60 of THE POWER OF A PRAYING PARENT.) What would you say is the opposite of pride? _____. The opposite of selfishness? _____
_____. Using all four of your answers, write down a prayer asking God to put those qualities in your child.

4. List the reasons you want your child to be obedient. (See the last paragraph on page 60 of THE POWER OF A PRAYING PARENT.)

5. Read Ephesians 6:10-13 and underline it in your Bible. Star verses 11 and 12. According to this scripture, are you in a battle with your children? _____. If not, against whom do you battle?

6. Read Nehemiah 9:26-27 and underline it in your Bible. According to this scripture, what does God do with His rebellious children? _____

_____.

What happens when they turn to God?

7. Do you ever see a rebellious spirit rise up in your child? _____. If so, how does it manifest it-self? _____.
Does it ever intimidate you? _____. Why or why not?

8. Do you believe that God has given you "authority over all the power of the enemy," including rebel-lion? _____. Do you for any reason feel

hesitant to stand against your child's enemy in prayer? _____. Why or why not?

9. Write a proclamation to the devil telling him that your child belongs to the Lord and no force of hell will be allowed to control him (her) with rebellion.

10. Pray out loud the prayer on pages 62–63 in THE POWER OF A PRAYING PARENT. Include specifics related to your child.

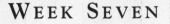

WEEK SEVEN

Read Chapter 7:
"Maintaining Good Family Relationships"
from THE POWER OF A PRAYING PARENT

1. Did you grow up with good, close family relationships? _____. Explain.

2. Do you have close family relationships now?
_____. Explain.

3. Is there any family situation that is strained, fractured, or severed? _____. Explain. Write out a prayer asking God to restore it.

4. Does your extended family or did your ancestors have a history of breached relationships? _____. Are there now or have there been people in your family who no longer speak to or see one another because of some kind of breakdown in their relationship? _____. Explain. How do you think that heritage might affect your child?

5. Read Romans 14:19 and underline it in your Bible. Are you willing to be the peacemaker in your family by praying for all damaged relationships to be restored? _____. Write to the Lord your commitment to that end.

6. Are you willing to tell the enemy that you will not allow family relationships in your child's life to be broken down? _____. Write it below as a proclamation.

7. Are there important relationships in your family which are especially crucial to your child's happiness? _____. List them below. Write out a prayer that your son (daughter) will have a lasting

and loving relationship with each one of these people.

8. Do you encourage your child to have a strong relationship with other members of your family? _____. Do you believe that feeling loved and accepted by other family members is crucial to your child's peace and happiness? _____. How could you pray to that end?

9. Read 1 Peter 3:8-9 and underline it in your Bible. Write out this scripture as a prayer over your child with regard to his (her) relationship with a specific family member.

10. Pray out loud the prayer on pages 67–68 in THE POWER OF A PRAYING PARENT. Include specifics about your family relationships.

WEEK EIGHT

Read Chapter 8:
"Attracting Godly Friends and Role Models"
from THE POWER OF A PRAYING PARENT

1. Read Proverbs 12:26 and underline it in your Bible. In light of this scripture, how important is it that your child have good, godly friends? _____. Why?

2. Is there anyone you consider to be a bad influence upon your child? _____. Is there anyone

who seems to bring out the worst in him (her)? _____. Explain.

3. Read Proverbs 13:20 in your Bible and underline it. Do you feel your child has any friends who are foolish? _____. What could happen if he (she) continues to spend time with those friends? Write out a prayer about them below.

4. Do you feel your child has friends who are wise? _____. Write out a prayer for those relationships to be strengthened.

5. Read 2 Corinthians 6:14-18 and underline it in your Bible. Does your child have any close relationships with non-believers? _____. What does the Bible say about that? How could you pray for those relationships?

6. Is there any relationship that is troubling or upsetting to your child? _____. Explain why. If you don't know, write out a prayer asking God to give you revelation about the cause of that strife and what to do about it.

7. Read Ephesians 4:31-32 and underline it in your Bible. Does your child easily forgive others? _____. In light of your answer, write out this scripture as a prayer over your child.

8. Who are the people your child looks up to in his (her) life? _____. Are they godly role models? _____. Write a

prayer below asking God to either strengthen those relationships or bring new ones into his (her) life.

9. Read Matthew 5:44 and underline it in your Bible. Write it out below as a prayer over your child. (I pray that *name of child* will love his (her) enemies...")

10. Pray out loud the prayer on pages 73–74 of THE POWER OF A PRAYING PARENT. Include specifics about your child's close friends and role models.

WEEK NINE

Read Chapter 9:
"Developing a Hunger for the Things of God"
from THE POWER OF A PRAYING PARENT

1. What does having a healthy fear of God mean? (See page 77 of THE POWER OF A PRAYING PARENT.)

2. What influences in your child's life are trying to draw his (her) attention away from the things of God?

3. Write out a prayer asking God to take away the desire for those things that compete with Him for your child's attention.

4. What are some of the things you can do to teach, instruct, train, and encourage your child in the things of God? (See page 78 of THE POWER OF A PRAYING PARENT for suggestions, but include your own specifics as well.)

5. Read Proverbs 10:27 and underline it in your Bible. In light of this scripture, what is the main reason you should pray for your child to reverence or fear God?

6. When our children develop a hunger for the things of God, they will know that the things of God are _____. They will become _____ and not _____. They will long for His _____, His _____, and His _____. They will _____ and live a _____.

(See page 78 of THE POWER OF A PRAYING PARENT.)

7. Read Psalm 34:8-10 and underline it in your Bible. What is promised for those who trust, fear, and seek the Lord?

8. Write Psalm 34:8-10 as a prayer for your child. ("Lord, I pray that _name of child_ will taste and see that You are good...")

9. How do you feel about your child's heart for God at this stage in his (her) life? _____ _____. Would you like to see your child have a greater hunger for the Lord? _____. Write out a prayer to that effect.

10. Pray out loud the prayer on pages 79–80 in THE POWER OF A PRAYING PARENT. Include specifics about your child's relationship with God.

WEEK TEN

Read Chapter 10: "Being the Person God Created"
from THE POWER OF A PRAYING PARENT

1. Do you believe your child ever compares himself
   (herself) unfavorably to others? _____.
   How so?

2. Do you ever compare yourself unfavorably to others?
   _____. If so, how might your doing so affect
   your child's attitude about himself (herself)?

3. Do you ever see your child striving to be something he (she) was not created to be, or straining to do something that will never fulfill him (her)? _____. Describe.

4. Write out a prayer asking God to reveal to your child the truth about who He created him (her) to be.

5. Write out a prayer asking God to reveal to you what your child's gifts and talents are. Write down what God shows you.

6. Write out a prayer asking God to reveal to you how to best nurture the gifts and talents He has placed in your child.

7. Read Isaiah 44:3-5 and underline it in your Bible. In verses 3 and 4, what are the rewards for the person who hungers and thirsts for more of the Lord?

_____

_____.

How will your desire for more of the Lord affect your child?

8. In verse 5 of the above scripture, what will the children say that is foundational to knowing who they are?

9. Does your child know with certainty that he (she) belongs to the Lord? _____. Write a prayer asking God to make that a reality in his (her) mind.

10. Pray out loud the prayer on pages 85–87 in THE POWER OF A PRAYING PARENT. Include specifics about your child.

WEEK ELEVEN

Read Chapter 11: "Following Truth, Rejecting Lies"
from THE POWER OF A PRAYING PARENT

1. Read Proverbs 12:22 and underline it in your Bible.
   How does God feel about lying? _____
   _____. How does He feel about
   people who tell the truth? _____
   _____.

2. Read Proverbs 21:6 and underline it in your Bible. In
   light of this scripture, what is the main reason that
   we must teach our children not to lie?

3. Do you believe lying is a serious offense against God?
   _____. Explain how serious you think it is.

4. How do you believe your own attitude toward lying affects your child?

5. What could you say to communicate to your child the seriousness of telling lies and the rewards of telling the truth?

6. Read John 14:15-17 and underline it in your Bible. Who is the Helper God gives us when we live His way? _____.
Write a prayer asking God to pour out His Spirit upon your child so that he (she) will receive the Spirit of Truth.

7. Read John 8:44 and underline it in your Bible. Who is the father of lies? _____.
When your child tells a lie, with whom has he (she) aligned himself (herself)? _____.
The more lies a child tells, the more he (she) gives place in his (her) heart to _____.
(See page 90 of THE POWER OF A PRAYING PARENT.)

8. Do you feel that your child already has a problem with lying? _____. Are you concerned that a tendency to lie might develop in the future? _____. Write out a proclamation stating that your child's heart belongs to God and no part of it will be surrendered to Satan, the father of lies.

9. Read Psalm 69:5 and underline it in your Bible. Write out a prayer asking God to reveal to you any time your child tells a lie, so that nothing will be hidden. Ask God to help you establish appropriate discipline when lying does occur, so that you will effectively communicate the seriousness of the offense.

10. Pray out loud the prayer on pages 92–93 of THE POWER OF A PRAYING PARENT. Include specifics about your child's ability to follow truth and reject lies.

WEEK TWELVE

Read Chapter 12:
"Enjoying a Life of Health and Healing"
from THE POWER OF A PRAYING PARENT

1. Read James 5:15-16 and underline it in your Bible. Put a star next to each verse. What does this scripture tell you to do if you or your child is sick? _____. What does God promise will happen when you do that?

2. Read Matthew 8:16-17 and underline it in your Bible. What did Isaiah prophesy that Jesus fulfilled? _____ _____.

Do you believe this is true for you and your child?

3. Does your child suffer from any physical ailment? _____. Are you concerned about any particular sickness developing or injury happening? _____. Describe these and write how you could pray on an ongoing basis for your child about these concerns.

4. Have you ever prayed for healing for your child? _____. What are some of the answers to prayer that you have seen as a result of you or others praying?

5. Read 2 Corinthians 5:7 and underline it in your Bible. Are you willing to continue to pray and believe for healing even when you don't see healing happening right away? _____. Why or why not?

6. Read Acts 14:8-10 and underline it in your Bible. What was the key to this man's healing?

7. When God looks upon you, does He see someone with faith enough to believe for healing? _____. Why or why not? _____ _____.

How would you like to pray about this?

8. Write a prayer below asking God to increase your faith to believe for healing in the people for whom you pray.

9. Write out a prayer asking God to give your child a faith strong enough to believe for God's healing power to flow on an ongoing basis through his (her) life.

10. Pray out loud the prayer on pages 97–98 in THE POWER OF A PRAYING PARENT. Include specifics about your child's health.

WEEK THIRTEEN

Read Chapter 13:
"Having the Motivation for Proper Body Care"
from THE POWER OF A PRAYING PARENT

1. Have you ever struggled with poor eating or exercise habits, smoking, drinking, or any other kind of neglect or abuse of your physical body? _____. Describe.

2. With regard to your previous answer, how different do you think you would be today if you'd had parents who prayed for you to have the discipline, self-control, and wisdom to be able to eat right, exercise regularly, and take good care of your body?_____. Explain.

3. Read 1 Corinthians 6:19-20 in your Bible and underline it. What is the temple of the Holy Spirit? _____. Do you believe that enough to see taking care of your temple as a ministry to God? _____. Explain why or why not.

4. What is God saying to you through 1 Corinthians
6:19-20? If you don't know, write out a prayer asking
Him to show you.

5. Write 1 Corinthians 6:19-20 as a prayer over yourself. ("Lord, I pray that You will help me to remember that my body is...")

6. Write 1 Corinthians 6:19-20 as a prayer over your child. (Lord, I pray that You will help <u>name of child</u> understand that his (her) body is...")

7. Have you noticed any tendency in your child to abuse his (her) physical body or neglect to care for it properly? Write out a prayer about it and be specific.

8. Read 1 Corinthians 10:31 and underline it in your Bible. How should you pray for your child's attitude in regard to taking care of his (her) physical health?

9. Read 1 Corinthians 3:17 and underline it in your Bible. In light of this scripture, why is it important to pray for your child to take care of his (her) body?

10. Pray out loud the prayer on pages 103–104 of THE POWER OF A PRAYING PARENT. Include specifics about your child. Pray it again over yourself if you feel the need to do so.

WEEK FOURTEEN

Read Chapter 14:
"Instilling the Desire to Learn"
from THE POWER OF A PRAYING PARENT

1. Read Proverbs 1:7 and underline it in your Bible.
   Where does knowledge begin? _____
   _____. What will your child become if
   he (she) refuses to learn? _____.
   Why is it important to teach your child to reverence
   God?

2. Read Proverbs 2:10-12 and underline it in your
   Bible. Describe why it is good to pray for wisdom for
   your child. Explain what could happen if you don't.

3. Read Proverbs 3:13-18 and underline it in your Bible. Why should you pray for your child to have wisdom? _____
_____. List the rewards that wisdom brings, and circle each one in your Bible.

4. Read Proverbs 3:21-24 and underline it in your Bible. What are the reasons you should pray for your child to have wisdom?

5. Read Proverbs 2:1-5 and underline it in your Bible. Write it out as a prayer over your child. (I pray that <u>name of child</u> will receive God's words and...")

6. What have you observed about your child's *ability* to learn? Be specific.

7. What have you observed about your child's *desire* to learn? Be specific.

8. In light of your answers to questions 6 and 7, write out a prayer about your child. Ask God to show you what you can do to help him (her).

9. Read Isaiah 54:13 and underline it in your Bible. Who is the ultimate teacher of your child? _____ _____. When God teaches your child, what does He promise to give him (her)? _____.

10. Pray out loud the prayer on pages 108–109 in THE POWER OF A PRAYING PARENT. Include specifics about your child's ability or desire to learn.

WEEK FIFTEEN

Read Chapter 15:
"Identifying God-Given Gifts and Talents"
from THE POWER OF A PRAYING PARENT

1. Do you feel you have God-given gifts or talents that would have been better developed if you'd had someone praying consistently for you? _____. Describe.

2. Read Romans 11:29 and underline it in your Bible. Even if you feel your God-given gifts and talents have not been developed to the fullest, what does

this scripture say about them? _____
_____.
What does that mean to you?

3. Do you observe any natural gifts, abilities, and talents in your child? _____. What are they?

4. Write out a prayer asking God to show you gifts and talents in your child that you have not seen before, or have seen but not with the clarity you would like.

5. Write out a prayer asking God to show you specifically how to best nurture, protect, and develop those
talents.

6. Read Proverbs 18:16 and underline it in your Bible.
Write out this scripture as a prayer for your child.
("Lord, I pray that the gifts and talents You have
placed in _name of child_ will make room...")

7. Read 1 Corinthians 1:4-7 and underline it in your Bible. Write it below as a prayer for your child. ("Thank You, God, concerning *name of child*, for that grace which was given to him (her) by Christ Jesus, that he (she) is being enriched in everything...")

8. Write out a prayer asking God to give you a glimpse of your child's potential for greatness. Include anything the Lord shows you.

9. Read Proverbs 22:29 and underline it in your Bible. Write out a prayer asking God to help your child excel in the gifts God has put in him (her), and for his (her) gifts to be recognized and appreciated by others.

10. Pray out loud the prayer on pages 114–115 in THE POWER OF A PRAYING PARENT. Include specifics about your child's gifts and talents.

WEEK SIXTEEN

Read Chapter 16: "Learning to Speak Life"
from THE POWER OF A PRAYING PARENT

1. Read Proverbs 13:3 and underline it in your Bible.
Why should you pray about the things that come out
of your child's mouth?

2. Words have power. We either can speak _____
or _____ into a situation. (See page 118 of
THE POWER OF A PRAYING PARENT.) Who does it hurt
the most when your child speaks words that are not
godly? _____.

3. Have you ever heard your child speak ungodly words? _____. If yes, how did you handle it? _____.
If no, how would you handle it if you did hear your child speak ungodly words?

4. Have you ever heard your child speak negative words about himself (herself)? _____. What did he (she) say and why do you believe those words were said?

5. Do you encourage your child to be open and honest about his (her) negative emotions and thoughts so you can pray with him (her) about them? _____. If your answer is yes, explain how you do that. If your answer is no, explain what you could do to encourage more open sharing.

6. Read Matthew 12:34-35 and underline it in your Bible. In light of this scripture, how could you pray for your child's heart?

7. Read Matthew 12:36-37 and underline it in your Bible. In light of this scripture, why should you pray for your child to speak godly words?

8. Read Psalm 19:14 and underline it in your Bible. Pray this scripture as a prayer over your child. ("Let the words of _name of child's_ mouth and the...")

9. A heart filled with _____ and the truth of _____ will produce godly speech that brings _____ _____.

   This is where our point of _____ should begin. (See page 119 of THE POWER OF A PRAYING PARENT.)

10. Pray out loud the prayer on pages 119–120 in THE POWER OF A PRAYING PARENT. Include specifics about your child's speech.

WEEK SEVENTEEN

Read Chapter 17:
"Staying Attracted to Holiness and Purity"
from THE POWER OF A PRAYING PARENT

1. Read Proverbs 20:11 and underline it in your Bible.
What do you want your child to be known for?

2. Do you feel you are a good role model for your child
as far as being someone who is attracted to holiness
and purity? _____. How would you like to
see that improve in your life?

3. Who is the real teacher of holiness and purity for
your child? _____. Holiness begins
with a love for _____. (See page 123 of THE
POWER OF A PRAYING PARENT.) In light of that, how
could you pray for your child?

4. The Bible says to "keep yourself pure," and that can
only be accomplished by total _____ ,
and the enabling _____.
(See page 123 of THE POWER OF A PRAYING PARENT.)
Write out a prayer about this for your child.

5. In order for your child to be attracted to holiness and purity, he (she) needs to see holiness and purity as attractive. Are there any people in your child's life who model that well? _____. If so, who are they? If no, write out a prayer asking God to bring those kind of people into your child's life.

6. Read 1 Thessalonians 4:7-8 and underline it in your Bible. Who calls us to holiness? _____. Who are we rejecting when we don't walk in holiness? _____. Write out a prayer asking God to help you communicate this to your child in a way he (she) can understand and receive.

7. Read 1 Timothy 4:12 and underline it in your Bible. Write this out as a prayer over your child. ("Lord, I pray that no one will despise *name of child*'s youth, but that he (she) will...")

8. Read Matthew 5:8 and underline it in your Bible. What kind of person is blessed? _____ _____. What is the blessing that person will receive? _____. In light of this scripture, how could you pray for your child?

9. Read Psalm 24:3-5 and underline it in your Bible. Write it out as a prayer over your child. ("I pray that *name of child* will ascend into the hill of the Lord and...")

10. Pray out loud the prayer on page 126 in THE POWER OF A PRAYING PARENT. Include specifics about your child's attitude toward living a holy and pure life.

WEEK EIGHTEEN

Read Chapter 18: "Praying Through a Child's Room"
from THE POWER OF A PRAYING PARENT

1. Read Deuteronomy 7:26 and underline it in your
   Bible. Put a star next to this verse. Why do you have
   to be concerned about what is in your child's room?

2. Read Psalm 101:2-3 and underline it in your Bible.
   Write it as a prayer over your child. ("Lord, I pray
   that *name of child* will behave wisely and in a perfect
   way. I pray he (she) will walk within his (her) house
   with a perfect heart...")

3. Read Joshua 24:15 and underline it in your Bible. Put a star next to it. Write the last sentence out below as a proclamation.

4. Write out the words, "As for me and my house, we will serve the Lord" (Joshua 24:25) on something and display it in your house. (My husband and I found a rock in our backyard, wrote this scripture on it with indelible ink, and set it on the hearth of our living room fireplace. You could do something as simple as writing it on a piece of paper and posting it on the refrigerator door.) There is more power in doing this than you can imagine. What did you write the verse on? _____. Where did you display it?

5. Does your child ever have nightmares, unexplained fears, or periods of aggressive behavior? _____. Explain.

6. Write out a prayer asking God to show you if there is anything unholy in your child's room, or anything that should not be in there. (For example, one of my friends prayed this prayer and God revealed to her that there was a stuffed animal in her young daughter's room that was scaring her and causing her to have nightmares. There didn't seem to be anything wrong with the stuffed animal, but it was not blessing this particular child. When she removed it, the nightmares stopped.)

7. Read Exodus 40:9 and underline it in your Bible. Have you ever anointed your child's room in that same way? _____. Why or why not?

8. If you have never anointed your child's room and prayed over it, would you be willing to do so now? _____. Write out a prayer asking God to break every yoke of the enemy and cleanse your child's room of anything unholy. Then pray it in the room.

9. In what ways would you like to see your child's room become a sanctuary to him (her)? Explain.

10. Pray out loud the prayer on page 132 in THE POWER OF A PRAYING PARENT. Include specifics about your child's room.

WEEK NINETEEN

Read Chapter 19: "Enjoying Freedom from Fear"
from THE POWER OF A PRAYING PARENT

1. What are your fears? Explain.

2. Do any of your fears manifest themselves in your
   child in any way? _____. How so?

3. What are your child's fears that you are aware of at this point?

4. Ask your child what fears he (she) has and list them below. If it is not possible to ask your child that question, write a prayer asking the Lord to reveal to you any fears in your child. Be sure and write down whatever He reveals.

5. Have you ever noticed fear gripping your child's heart so that he (she) becomes unreasonable? According to Luke 10:19, over whom and what has Jesus given us authority? _____.

Where does a spirit of fear come from? _____
_____. Does it come from God?
_____. Do you have the power and authority
through Jesus Christ to resist a spirit of fear on your
child's behalf? _____. Does fear have power
over your child? _____. Do you have power
over fear? _____. Can fear and the presence
of the Lord coexist? _____. (See page
136 of THE POWER OF A PRAYING PARENT.)

6. Read 1 John 4:18 and underline it in your Bible. In
   light of this scripture, how could you pray for your
   child with regard to fear?

7. Read Psalm 27:1 and underline it in your Bible. Write it out as a declaration of truth over your child. (The Lord is *name of child's* light and salvation...")

8. Read Psalm 91:4-6 and underline it in your Bible. Put a star next to each verse. Write it out as a prayer to speak over your child. ("Lord, I pray that you would cover *name of child* with your feathers and underneath your wings may he (she)...") Speak this over your child whenever he (she) is afraid.

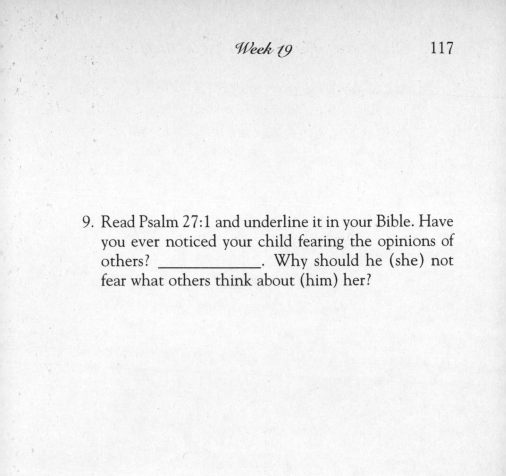

9. Read Psalm 27:1 and underline it in your Bible. Have you ever noticed your child fearing the opinions of others? _____. Why should he (she) not fear what others think about (him) her?

10. Pray out loud the prayer on page 137 of THE POWER OF A PRAYING PARENT. Include specifics about your child's fears.

WEEK TWENTY

Read Chapter 20: "Receiving a Sound Mind"
from THE POWER OF A PRAYING PARENT

1. Does your child ever struggle with confusion, the in-
   ability to stay focused, difficulty understanding
   things appropriate for his (her) age, or negative
   thinking? _____. Describe.

2. Do you have any concerns or fears about the devel-
   opment of your child's mind? _____. What
   are they? _____.

_____

_____.

Why do you have those concerns?

3. Does your child have a tendency to be too self-
   focused? _____. Praising God is the best
   way to combat self-centeredness. How could you
   pray about this for your child?

4. Read Isaiah 26:3 and underline it in your Bible. Put
   a star next to it. According to this scripture, what
   should your child be focused on? _____
   _____. How could you pray about that?

5. Read Philippians 2:5 and underline it in your Bible. According to this scripture, how do we get the mind of Christ? _____

    _____.

    Does it have to do with a choice we make? _____

    _____. How could you pray about this for your child?

6. Read 1 Corinthians 2:14-16 and underline it in your Bible. Can the natural man receive the things of the Spirit of God? _____. Why or why not?

    _____

    _____.

    When we receive Jesus and have the Holy Spirit in us, we have the mind of _____.

7. Read Romans 1:21 and underline it in your Bible. Bad things happened to these believers because they did not _____ and they were not _____. As a result, what were the bad things that happened to them? _____, _____, and _____. Why should you pray for your child to learn to praise God and be thankful to Him?

8. Read Romans 8:6 and underline it in your Bible. What kind of mind brings death? _____ _____. What kind of mind brings life and peace? _____ _____. What should you then pray for your child?

9. Read 2 Timothy 1:7 and underline it in your Bible. Put a star next to it. Write it as a proclamation over your child. ("God has not given <u>name of child</u> a spirit of fear...") Speak it out loud to or over your child.

10. Pray out loud the prayer on pages 143–144 of THE POWER OF A PRAYING PARENT. Include specifics about your child.

WEEK TWENTY-ONE

Read Chapter 21: "Inviting the Joy of the Lord"
from THE POWER OF A PRAYING PARENT

1. When you observe your child's face, does it most often reflect peace and joy, or is it frequently depressed, angry, sad, moody, or troubled? Describe.

2. Read Psalm 16:11 and underline it in your Bible. Where do we find joy? _____.

Write this scripture as a prayer over your child. ("Lord, I pray that You will show *name of child* the path of life...")

3. Read Romans 15:13 and underline it in your Bible. Write this as a prayer over your child. ("Lord, I pray that You, the God of hope, will fill *name of child* with all joy and peace...")

4. Read Psalm 118:24 and underline it in your Bible. Write this scripture out as a prayer over your child.

("Lord, I know that this is the day that You have made for *name of child*. I pray that he (she) will...")

5. Joy doesn't have to do with _____
_____; it has to do with looking
into _____ and knowing
_____. (See page 148
of THE POWER OF A PRAYING PARENT.)

6. Read Galatians 5:22-23 and underline it in your
Bible. Write out a prayer asking God to manifest
each of these in your child. List each fruit of the
Spirit specifically.

7. Read Philippians 4:11 and underline it in your Bible. In light of this scripture, how could you pray for your child?

8. Read Proverbs 15:15 and underline it in your Bible. In light of this scripture, what happens to someone with a joyful attitude? _____

_____.

How could you pray about that for your child?

9. Read Numbers 6:24-26 and underline it in your Bible. Write it out as a prayer over your child. ("Lord, I pray that You would bless _name of child_ and keep him (her)...")

10. Pray out loud the prayer on page 149 in THE POWER OF A PRAYING PARENT. Include specifics about your child's attitude.

WEEK TWENTY-TWO

Read Chapter 22:
"Destroying an Inheritance of Family Bondage"
from THE POWER OF A PRAYING PARENT

1. Is there any trait, characteristic, or habit you or your
   husband have which you would not like to see your
   child emulate or inherit? _____. Describe.

2. Is there any negative tendency that seems to run in your family or your spouse's family that you would not like to see your child inherit (for instance, laziness, irresponsibility, self-pity, anger, unforgiveness, bitterness, gossiping, coldness, being critical)? _____. Describe.

3. Are there any sinful or destructive patterns of behavior on either side of your child's family which you would not want to touch your child's life (alcoholism, infidelity, lying, divorce, drugs)? _____. Describe.

4. God has given you authority over all the power of the enemy. Take that authority and write out a prayer breaking all the bondages over your family that you listed in questions 1, 2, and 3. ("In the name of Jesus, I break the spirit of divorce and alcoholism and I say that it has no part in my life or the life of my child...")

5. Read Romans 8:15-17 and underline it in your Bible. Whose child are you? _____.
Where does your inheritance ultimately come from? _____. Where does your child's inheritance ultimately come from? _____.

6. Write out Romans 8:15-17 as a proclamation to the enemy of your child's soul, and inform him that your child's inheritance comes from the Lord.

7. Read 1 John 1:9 and underline it in your Bible. How do we become cleansed of the effects of sin?_____ _____. Once we do that, what does God do? _____ _____. In light of that, how should you pray for your child?

8. Read Galatians 5:1 in your Bible and underline it. Write it as a prayer over yourself and your child.

9. Read 2 Corinthians 5:17. Write out this scripture as a proclamation over your child, and then speak it out loud over your child. *"Name of child* is in Christ and he (she) is a new creation...")

10. Pray out loud the prayer on pages 155–156 of THE POWER OF A PRAYING PARENT. Include specifics about your child.

WEEK TWENTY-THREE

Read Chapter 23:
"Avoiding Alcohol, Drugs, and Other Addictions"
from THE POWER OF A PRAYING PARENT

1. Read Proverbs 11:3 and underline it in your Bible. In light of this scripture, what would be a good character trait for your child to have in order to be able to resist any temptation that the enemy puts in his (her) path? _____. Write out a prayer for your child regarding that.

2. One of the best ways to shield your child from temptation is to pray that he (she) be built up in the truth of the Lord. Write out a prayer to that effect for your child.

3. Read 1 John 4:2-4 and underline it in your Bible. How do you know that a spirit is of God? _____ _____. How do you know that a spirit is *not* of God? _____ _____. The spirit in you is from _____. The spirit in the world is from _____. Which spirit is greater? _____.

4. Do you believe you have authority over all the power of the enemy? (Luke 10:19) _____. Do you, then, have power over the enemy of your child? _____. Do you believe you have the power to

break strongholds in your child's life through prayer?
_____. Why or why not?

5. Read 1 Corinthians 10:13 and underline it in your
   Bible. Write it out as a prayer over your child. ("No
   temptation has overtaken *name of child* except such
   as is common to man...")

6. Read Romans 8:13 and underline it in your Bible.
   Write this as a prayer over your child. ("Lord, I pray

that _name of child_ will not live according to the flesh
which brings death, but will…")

7. Read Deuteronomy 30:19-20 and underline it in
   your Bible. In light of this scripture, how important
   is it that your child make the right choices? What
   can happen if he (she) doesn't?

8. In Deuteronomy 30:20, what three things must your
   child do in order to have a long life? _____
   _____, _____
   _____, and _____
   _____. Write out a prayer
   asking God to help your child learn to do those
   things.

9. Write out a prayer asking the Holy Spirit to help your child make right choices, choices for life, every day.

10. Pray out loud the prayer on pages 160–161 in THE POWER OF A PRAYING PARENT. Include specifics about your child's ability to resist temptation of any kind.

WEEK TWENTY-FOUR

Read Chapter 24: "Rejecting Sexual Immorality"
from THE POWER OF A PRAYING PARENT

1. Read 1 Peter 2:11 and underline it in your Bible. Are the consequences of sexual sin manifested only in the body? _____. Where else in your child will there be damage from sexual sin? _____ _____. From your own experience or the experience of others you know, can you think of an example where wholeness of the soul was sacrificed because of giving place to the lust of the flesh? _____. Explain.

2. When we or our children have sexual sin in our lives, the fullness of _____,
_____, _____,
and _____ is sacrificed.
(See page 164 of THE POWER OF A PRAYING PARENT.)

3. Read Proverbs 28:26 and underline it in your Bible. In light of this scripture, how should we pray for our children?

4. Read James 1:12 and underline it in your Bible. Write this as a prayer over your child's life. Remember that even if your child has already stumbled into sexual immorality, you can pray for him (her) to live in sexual purity from now on.

5. Are you convinced of the need for sexual purity in your life and the lives of your children? _____. Explain why or why not.

6. Write out a prayer for yourself that you will never succumb to a trap of the enemy and fall into sexual immorality, including your thought life. (If there is any sexual immorality you have committed, speak a confession of it to the Lord so that the enemy has no grounds to have a place in your life.)

7. Read James 1:14-15 and underline it in your Bible. According to this scripture, how could your child be tempted? _____

_____.

What can happen if he (she) is?

8. Read Galatians 5:16-21 and underline it in your Bible. How are we to walk? _____.
How are we not to walk? _____.
List the works of the flesh and pray that your child avoid each one. Even a small child can manifest a seed that could grow into any one of these if it is not stamped out in prayer.

9. Read Galatians 5:22-23 and underline it in your
Bible. Write out a prayer asking God to help your
child exhibit all of these fruits of the Spirit. Mention
each one specifically.

10. Pray out loud the prayer on pages 165–166 in THE
POWER OF A PRAYING PARENT. Include specifics about
your child.

WEEK TWENTY-FIVE

Read Chapter 25: "Finding the Perfect Mate"
from THE POWER OF A PRAYING PARENT

1. Read Psalm 127:1 and underline it in your Bible. According to this scripture, why is it important that your child hear from God about who he (she) is to marry?

2. Read Malachi 2:13-16 and underline verse 16 in your Bible. Why were the people crying at the altar of the Lord? _____
_____.
Why did God no longer accept their offering? _____
_____.

Why does He make a husband and wife to be one?
_____.

How does God feel about divorce and why?

3. Read Proverbs 12:26 and underline it in your Bible. In light of this scripture, how should you pray for your child's relationships? Remember, marriages begin as simple relationships.

4. Read 2 Corinthians 6:14 and underline it in your Bible. What kind of mate do you need to pray for your child to marry? _____.
Write out a prayer for your child to that effect.

5. Read 1 John 1:7 and underline it in your Bible. In order for your child to have the kind of close relationship needed to make a marriage work, what does he (she) need to have in common with his (her) mate? _____.
Write out a prayer to that effect.

6. Has there been divorce anywhere in your family? If so, write out a prayer asking God to break that spirit over your family. If no, ask God to keep it far from you.

7. The spirit of _____ keeps a marriage
   together. A spirit of _____ destroys
   a marriage. (See page 170 in THE POWER OF A
   PRAYING PARENT.) Write out a prayer asking God to
   be in charge of your child's marriage, and that there
   be no divorce in his (her) future.

8. Write out a prayer that your child not only find the
   perfect mate, but that he (she) will not enter into
   marriage with expectations so high that his (her)
   spouse can't live up to them.

9. Read Colossians 1:9 and underline it in your Bible. Write out what Paul prayed here for the Colossians as a prayer over your child. Then pray for God to reveal His will to your child regarding his (her) future mate. ("I do not cease to pray for <u>*name of child*</u> and ask that he (she) may be filled with...")

10. Pray out loud the prayer on pages 171–172 in THE POWER OF A PRAYING PARENT. Include specifics about your child's future or present mate.

Read Chapter 26: "Living Free of Unforgiveness"
from THE POWER OF A PRAYING PARENT

1. Does forgiveness flow freely in your family or does unforgiveness have a place in one or more family members?
_____. Explain.

2. Do you have any unforgiveness that you need to confess so you can be set free of it? _____. If so, write out a prayer asking God to help you forgive.

If not, write out a prayer asking God to reveal any hidden unforgiveness in you, and to keep you free from unforgiveness in the future.

3. Does your child find it easy to forgive or hard to let go of unforgiveness? _____. Explain your observations.

4. Write a prayer asking God to show you any specific point of unforgiveness in your child. Then write down anything the Lord reveals.

5. How could you pray specifically *with* your child about unforgiveness in his (her) life? Write it out as a prayer.

6. Read Matthew 6:14-15 and underline it in your Bible. Why should you pray for your child to be a forgiving person?

7. Read Ephesians 4:31-32 and underline it in your Bible. Write this as a prayer over your child. ("Lord, I pray that *name of child* will let all bitterness, wrath...")

8. Read 1 Corinthians 13:4-7 and underline it in your Bible. Write it out as a prayer over your child. ("Lord, I pray that *name of child* will have the kind of love that suffers long and is kind...")

9. Read Colossians 3:12-13 and underline it in your Bible. Write this as a prayer over your child. ("Lord, I pray that *name of child*, who is your holy and beloved child, will put on tender mercies...")

10. Pray out loud the prayer on pages 178–179 in THE POWER OF A PRAYING PARENT. Include specifics about your child.

WEEK TWENTY-SEVEN

Read Chapter 27: "Walking in Repentance"
from THE POWER OF A PRAYING PARENT

1. Read Proverbs 28:13 and underline it in your Bible.
   What happens to someone who covers up his (her)
   sin? _____.
   What should your child be encouraged to do instead?

   _____

   _____. Why?

2. Parents can usually recognize a look of guilt on a
   child's face. Have you ever seen that look on your
   child's face? _____. Whether you have or

not, write a prayer asking God to keep your child from ever becoming comfortable with concealing his (her) sins.

3. Read 1 John 3:21-22 and underline it in your Bible. If your child confesses his (her) sin, what will he (she) experience?

4. Have you ever detected sin on your child's face before you discovered it in his (her) behavior? _____

_____. Describe. Do you feel God revealed that to you?

5. Read Psalm 69:5 and underline it in your Bible. Even if your child can hide his (her) sins from you, can they be hidden from God? _____. Do you believe that when you pray, God will reveal your child's sins to you? _____. Why or why not?

6. Your child must be encouraged to admit or confess his (her) sin. But he (she) must also be repentant, or sorry enough to not want to do it again. Write out

the kind of prayer you would like for your child to pray that includes confession, repentance, and seeking forgiveness from God.

7. Do you think your child would be willing to pray such a prayer? _____. Why or why not? _____ _____. How could you pray about that?

8. Read Psalm 139:23-24 and underline it in your Bible. Write it out as a prayer over your child. ("Search *name of child*, O God, and know his (her) heart...")

9. Read Psalm 51:10-12 and underline it in your Bible. Write it out as a prayer over your child. ("Create in *name of child* a clean heart O God...")

10. Pray out loud the prayer on pages 183–184 of THE POWER OF A PRAYING PARENT. Include specifics about your child.

WEEK TWENTY-EIGHT

Read Chapter 28:
"Breaking Down Ungodly Strongholds"
from THE POWER OF A PRAYING PARENT

1. Have you ever observed something in your child that you thought was not right, but you didn't have any hard evidence to support it? How did it manifest itself and what did you do about it?

2. Read Luke 12:2 and underline it in your Bible. How does this verse inspire you to pray for your child?

3. Write out a prayer asking God to always reveal to you the truth of what is going on in your child's mind and life.

4. Do you ever see your child following a pattern of misbehavior (dishonesty, deception, greed, selfishness, arrogance, disobedience)? _____. If so,

describe what you see. If not, write a prayer asking God to reveal anything you need to see.

5. The devil always seeks to establish his rulership in our children's lives. Whether you see anything like that in your child or not, write out a prayer asking God to destroy any strongholds the enemy wants to establish in your child's life.

6. Read Matthew 6:13 and underline it in your Bible. Write this scripture as a prayer over your child.

7. You don't have to be suspicious of your _____ _____, but you do have to be suspicious of _____ who is waiting to erect a _____ in his (her) life. (See page 189 of THE POWER OF A PRAYING PARENT.)

8. Read 1 Peter 5:8-9 and underline it in your Bible. What are you supposed to do when the devil seeks to devour your child? _____

_____.

What is the best way you can think of to resist the devil's plans for your child?

9. What does the instruction to be sober, vigilant, and steadfast mean to you with regard to praying for your child to be protected from the enemy's plans? (See 1 Peter 5:8.)

10. Pray out loud the prayer on pages 190–191 in THE POWER OF A PRAYING PARENT. Include specifics about your child.

WEEK TWENTY-NINE

Read Chapter 29: "Seeking Wisdom and Discernment" from THE POWER OF A PRAYING PARENT

1. Read James 1:5 and underline it in your Bible. What is the promise to you in this verse?

2. Do you ever have concerns about your child's ability to make right choices and good decisions? _____. Explain.

3. Do you believe you can ask God for wisdom for your child? _____. Why or why not?

4. Read Proverbs 2:10-12 and underline it in your Bible. Write it as a prayer over your child. ("Lord, I pray that wisdom will be in ̅n̅a̅m̅e̅ ̅o̅f̅ ̅c̅h̅i̅l̅d̅'̅s̅ heart...")

5. Read Proverbs 3:13-18 and underline it in your Bible. List below all the benefits of someone who has wisdom.

6. Read Proverbs 4:7-9 and underline it in your Bible. According to this scripture, what is the main thing we need? _____.
What else? _____.
What are the benefits of having wisdom and understanding?

7. Read Proverbs 23:24-25 and underline it in your Bible. As a parent, what is the benefit for you if your child has wisdom?

8. Read Proverbs 2:1-7 and underline it in your Bible. List the ways you can obtain wisdom and discernment (receive God's Word, treasure God's commands).

9. Write out Proverbs 2:1-7 as a prayer for your child. ("Lord, I pray that *name of child* will receive Your Word and treasure Your commands within him (her). May he (she)...")

10. Pray out loud the prayer on page 195 in THE POWER OF A PRAYING PARENT. Include specifics about your child.

WEEK THIRTY

Read Chapter 30: "Growing in Faith"
from THE POWER OF A PRAYING PARENT

1. For his (her) age, do you feel your child has a strong faith, a weak faith, or somewhere in between? _____.

   Explain.

2. Explain what kind of faith you would like to see your child have.

3. Does your child have self-motivation and a sense of purpose? _____. Explain.

4. Read Mark 9:23 and underline it in your Bible. Put a star next to this verse. Write it below. Take a moment to memorize it. At the first opportunity, teach it to your child and speak it whenever you can.

5. Sensing our limitations does not mean we have no _____. It's feeling that _____ _____ has limitations that indicates a _____.

(See page 200 in THE POWER OF A PRAYING PARENT.)

6. Children who have strong faith exhibit distinctly different characteristics from those who do not. Can you think of some of them? List them below. Does your child exhibit faith, or lack of faith, in any particular way? Explain.

7. Read James 1:6-8 and underline it in your Bible. Describe what it is like for a doubter.

8. Read 1 Corinthians 13:13 and underline it in your Bible. What are the three things that will be lasting in your child's life? _____, _____ and _____.

Write a prayer asking God to give your child all three of these.

9. Do you struggle with doubt or do you have a strong faith? _____. What kind of faith would you like to have? _____. How would you like to pray about this for yourself?

10. Pray out loud the prayer on pages 203–204 in THE POWER OF A PRAYING PARENT. Include specifics about your child's faith.

Answers to Prayer

*B*e sure to record every answer to prayer you receive for your child. You can start here, but you are going to run out of room before long. Remember, after you acknowledge what God has done, be sure to thank Him for it.

_____

_____

_____

_____

_____

_____

_____

_____

_____

_____

_____

_____

Answers to Prayer

Answers to Prayer

Answers to Prayer

Answers to Prayer

Answers to Prayer

Answers to Prayer

Answers to Prayer

OTHER BOOKS by STORMIE OMARTIAN

The Power of a Praying® Wife

The Power of a Praying® Wife

The Power of a Praying® Wife
Audio Book

The Power of a Praying® Wife
Book of Prayers

The Power of a Praying® Wife
Prayer & Study Guide

The Power of a Praying® Wife
Deluxe Edition

The Power of a Praying® Woman

The Power of a Praying® Woman

The Power of a Praying® Woman Bible

The Power of a Praying® Woman
Book of Prayers

The Power of a Praying® Woman
Prayer & Study Guide

The Power of a Praying® Woman
Deluxe Edition

The Power of a Praying® Husband

The Power of a Praying® Husband

The Power of a Praying® Husband
Book of Prayers

The Power of a Praying® Husband
Prayer & Study Guide

The Power of a Praying® Parent

The Power of a Praying® Parent

The Power of a Praying® Parent
Book of Prayers

The Power of a Praying® Parent
Prayer & Study Guide

The Power of a Praying® Parent
Deluxe Edition

Just Enough Light for the Step I'm On

Just Enough Light for the Step I'm On

Just Enough Light for the Step I'm On...
A Devotional Prayer Journey

Just Enough Light for the Step I'm On
Book of Prayers

The Prayer That Changes Everything®

The Prayer That Changes Everything®

The Prayer That Changes Everything®
Book of Prayers

The Prayer That Changes Everything®
Prayer Cards

The Prayer That Changes Everything®
Audio Book

Praying Through the Deeper Issues of Marriage

Praying Through the Deeper Issues
of Marriage

Praying Through the Deeper Issues
of Marriage Audio Book

Praying Through the Deeper Issues
of Marriage Book of Prayers

Praying Through the Deeper Issues
of Marriage Prayer & Study Guide

Other Items

A Book of Prayer

Greater Health God's Way

Stormie

The Power of Praying®

The Power of Praying® Together

The Power of a Praying® Nation

For this Child I Prayed

Praying Through the Bible

Prayers for Emotional Wholeness

The Power of a Praying® Teen

The Power of a Praying® Kid

What Happens when I Talk to God?

The Power of Praying® Gift Collection